# The Mists of Eden

## NATURE'S LAST PARADISE

# The Mists of

## LANDMARK EDITIONS, INC.

P.O. Box 270169 • 1402 Kansas Avenue • Kansas City, Missouri 64127
(816)241-4919

# Eden
## NATURE'S LAST PARADISE

*Written and Illustrated by*
## Erica Sherman

Dedicated to:
my mom and dad
for their loving support;
Mrs. Jerri Shearer
and Mrs. Laurel Pettit
for their guidance;
all my teachers for their
encouragement and understanding;
and especially to the inhabitants
of the rainforests whose
future survival depends upon
the efforts of us all.

COPYRIGHT © 1998 BY ERICA SHERMAN

International Standard Book Number: 0-933849-69-9 (LIB.BDG.)

Library of Congress Cataloging-in-Publication Data
Sherman, Erica, 1985-
    The mists of Eden: nature's last paradise /
written and illustrated by Erica Sherman.
    p.   cm.
    Summary:  The rainforest, nature's last paradise, speaks of its waters,
its plants and animals, and its struggle to survive being destroyed by people.
ISBN 0-933849-69-9 (lib.bdg. : alk. paper)
    1. Rain forests—Juvenile poetry.    2. Nature—Juvenile poetry.
    3. Children's poetry, American.
    [1. Rain forests—Poetry.
    2. Conservation of natural resources—Poetry.
    3.  American poetry.]

    I. Title.
PS3569.H424M57      1998
811'.54—dc21                                              98-14468
                                                         CIP
                                                         AC

Creative Coordinator:  David Melton
Editorial Coordinator:  Nancy R. Thatch
Production Assistant:   Brian Hubbard

Printed in the United States of America

Landmark Editions, Inc.
P.O. Box 270169
1402 Kansas Avenue
Kansas City, Missouri 64127
(816) 241-4919

Visit our Website — www.LandmarkEditions.com

# THE MISTS OF EDEN
## Nature's Last Paradise

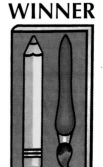
The special interests of young people often become the topics of the books they create. Some of Landmark's previous winning books: *Who Owns the Sun?*; *Oliver and the Oil Spill*; *Life in the Ghetto*; and *Jambi and the Lions* were born out of the special interests of the students who wrote and illustrated them.

Erica Sherman's interest and concern for the survival of the tropical rainforests of the world motivated her to write and illustrate her extraordinary book.

THE MISTS OF EDEN is a visually stunning book, filled with vibrant colors and beautiful images. The free verse Erica has written is lyrical and lovely, and her poetic stanzas become important extensions of her beautiful paintings. The factual statements she presents offer readers additional information about the world's vital need for these rainforests and the impending threats that could destroy them. As the book progresses, these statements become counterpoints that make her poetry and illustrations more meaningful and thought provoking.

Together, Erica's paintings, her poetry, and the factual statements build to a final impact that is chilling and alarming indeed.

This was not an easy book for Erica to develop. All the pieces had to fit together and become a part of the whole. The idea of allowing the "voice" of the poetic narrative to come from the rainforest was a very wise one. It offered Erica the opportunity to "speak" to her readers in a more personal and emotional way.

The quality of her work as an artist is truly amazing. I have worked with thousands of students who were from six to ninety-eight years of age. I have seen outstanding works come from young writers and artists. But I have never seen another thirteen-year-old who could paint with the skills and precision of Erica Sherman.

The result of Erica's creative skills is a powerful book — powerfully beautiful and powerfully profound.

Now — you are about to enter THE MISTS OF EDEN and be amazed and emotionally touched by the talents of a very young, but very accomplished writer and illustrator.

> — David Melton
> Creative Coordinator
> Landmark Editions, Inc.

Through the mists that surround me,
my leafy arms reach out to greet the morning sun.
Here I stand, as I have stood for millions of years —
living, breathing, evolving, growing.

Tropical rainforests often are called the "lungs of the world." The leaves of their plants and trees constantly absorb carbon dioxide from the atmosphere and convert it into enormous amounts of clean oxygen for the world to breathe.

*I am a rainforest —*
*a tropical Eden —*
*nature's last paradise on Earth.*

Tropical rainforests are always warm and moist because they grow on lands that lie on or near the equator and receive more than 80 inches of rainfall a year. The moisture their leaves release into the air forms billowing clouds that promote rainfall and affect weather patterns around the world.

As the veils of mist fade away,
golden rays of sunlight filter
through my canopy of emerald green.
From the tops of my towering trees
to the depths of my flowing rivers,
an abundance of life begins to stir.

*Another day has dawned,*
*and the age-old cycle of survival begins anew.*

More than half of the world's species of plants and animals live in rainforests, and half of those are found in the *canopies.* A *canopy* is made up of the thick upper foliage of the tallest trees that grow 65 to 200 feet high. It is truly the heart of a rainforest where 90 percent of *photosynthesis* occurs when the green leaves use the energy of sunlight to convert water and carbon dioxide into basic plant food. The nourished *canopy* trees can then bear flowers, fruits, nuts, and seeds that feed thousands of species of insects, birds, and other animals.

9

Sweet are the songs of my birds
that fill the air with music.
They call distant chants to the fading night
and sing ancient hymns to the morning light.
The vibrant rhythms of their melodic songs
are the heartbeat of my jungle.

10

*Soaring high in graceful flight*
*or sitting proudly in regal splendor,*
*their bright feathers add majesty to my kingdom.*

The Amazon is the largest rainforest on Earth. It is home to nearly half of all the world's species of birds, including large, colorful parrots and toucans. The rainforests in Central America offer safe havens to at least 225 kinds of birds during their migration to and from North and South America.

Soft, silky petals open wide,
spreading delightful fragrances
throughout my primeval landscape.
Their brilliant bursts of color invite
hummingbirds and brightly painted butterflies
to hover near and dine on sweet nectar.

*Soon these welcome guests fly away,*
*carrying pollen to other flowers that bloom*
*in the gardens of my wilderness.*

Hummingbirds are found only in North, Central, and South America. Of the 163 known species of hummingbirds, most live in tropical rainforests. The largest and most colorful butterflies are found in tropical areas, too. In the Amazon rainforest alone, there are more species of butterflies than anywhere else in the world.

The smallest of my creatures are
by far the largest in number.
From beneath my darkened soil
to the heights of my tallest trees,
multitudes of insects are everywhere —
marching, swarming, scurrying, foraging.

*In the warmth of my eternal summer,*
*my canopy trees, laden with lush bromeliads,*
*offer food and shelter to a myriad of creatures.*

In such a warm climate, insects reproduce several times a year and multiply greatly. One canopy tree can contain more than 50 species of ants and 10,000 species of other insects, spiders, and mites. Insects and other animals feed on, pollinate, and fertilize the bromeliads and other "air plants" that grow on the trunks and limbs of the trees.

Gentle are my quiet streams
that wander lazily like winding dreams.
Mighty are my rivers swift
that surge forward with defiant force.
Thunderous are my waterfalls
that leap from rocky ledges

*and plunge fearlessly to depths below.*
*They are the carriers of my life-giving waters*
*to all living things that dwell within my domain.*

The Amazon River is approximately 4,000 miles long. It has more than one thousand tributaries flowing into it. Its gigantic system of rivers, streams, creeks, flooded rainforests, lagoons, and swamps carry a greater volume of water than any other river in the world, even more than the Mississippi, Nile, and Yangtze rivers combined.

In an ebb and flow of liquid haze,
underwater ballets are performed in silent grace.
Fish swim by in synchronized harmony.
As they glide through my watery realm,
their tranquil movements create lovely images —
so peaceful, so calm, so serene.

*But their safe passage is only an illusion,
for within the quiet beauty of my waters
there are ever-present dangers.*

More kinds of fish live in the Amazon River than in the Atlantic Ocean. In the rainy season, the river floods large areas of the rainforest to the tops of its trees. Many fish swim among the submerged trees and eat the flowers, fruits, nuts, seeds, and insects found there. That is why they are called the "fish of the trees."

Slowly and silently, a cayman patrols
my murky waters in search of easy prey.
A constrictor coils around the trunk of a tree,
poised, ready to kill with its deadly embrace.
Frogs may appear to be defenseless.

But beware! Their colorful coats may warn

of powerful poisons hidden beneath.
Survival is for the strongest,
the fittest, and the most alert.

There are many cold-blooded reptiles and amphibians in warm tropical rainforests. In the lowlands of the Amazon, more than 270 known species of reptiles and 300 kinds of frogs live in or near muddy shallow waters, sluggish rivers, and open swamps and marshes.

Many exotic mammals roam
the wide expanse of my untamed lands.
The gentle ones sample the fruits of my trees
and nibble the leaves of my plants.
Others, more cunning and fierce,
search the shadows and lie in wait for their prey.

*Only the jaguars feel no fear,*
*for they have no predators.*
*They reign supreme in my jungle.*

Tropical rainforests are home to many unusual mammals that cannot be found anywhere else in the world, including the slow-moving sloth. The Amazon rainforest contains approximately 350 species of mammals, ranging from the world's smallest monkey, the pygmy marmoset, to the world's largest rodent, the *capybara*.

My native people live in harmony with nature.
They understand and respect my ways.
With gratefulness, they accept
the gifts of life I offer.
With wisdom, they take only
as much as they need to survive.

*But now, others have entered my territory —*
*outsiders who come only to take and to destroy.*
*They do not care about my delicate balance of nature.*

Since 1900 more than one third of the Amazon tribes have died out. Many of their people were killed by diseases brought in by outsiders. If all the Indians perish, the world will lose the special knowledge these natives have about the rainforest's animals, and also its plants, which are the world's most bountiful sources of lifesaving medicines.

*Invaders stalk me night and day*
*with mighty saws and slashing jaws.*
*Every minute, every hour, bit by bit,*
*they cut into me and tear away my life,*
*moving closer and closer to my heart.*
*Then they light torches and set me on fire.*

*I stand in silent pain as flames leap up around me.*
*I am suffocated in shrouds of endless smoke*
*and left with blackened scars across my lands.*

Each year 55,000 square miles of tropical rainforests are cut or burned to clear land for farming, ranching, and logging. Since 1949 more than 49 percent of these rainforests have disappeared forever, and as a result, more than 50 species of plants and animals become extinct every day.

In the time it takes you to snap your fingers once, another whole acre of rainforest will have been destroyed.

What is to become of me —
my plants, my animals, my people?
All that nature has carefully made,
All her songs and serenades,
All the wonders that I hold,
All my secrets yet untold,
Are all to perish in the mists of Eden
and be buried in unmarked graves?

*Oh, people of the Earth,*
*Hear my cry!*
*Before it is too late,*
*Help me survive!*
*Do not let me die!*

If the people of the Earth allow all tropical rainforests to be destroyed, we will lose our most important supply of oxygen, our greatest source of pharmaceutical medicines, and cures for deadly diseases. More species of plants and animals will become extinct. And gone forever will be some of the most beautiful and fascinating areas of the world.

# BOOKS FOR STUDENTS BY STUDENTS

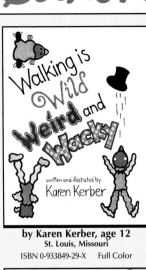

**Walking is Wild Weird and Wacky**
written and illustrated by Karen Kerber

by Karen Kerber, age 12
St. Louis, Missouri
ISBN 0-933849-29-X    Full Color

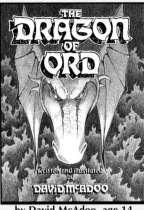

**THE DRAGON OF ORD**
written and illustrated by DAVID McADOO

by David McAdoo, age 14
Springfield, Missouri
ISBN 0-933849-23-0    Inside Duotone

**Strong and Free**
written and illustrated by Amy Hagstrom

by Amy Hagstrom, age 9
Portola, California
ISBN 0-933849-15-X    Full Color

**ME AND MY VEGGIES**
WRITTEN AND ILLUSTRATED BY ISAAC WHITLATCH

by Isaac Whitlatch, age 1[?]
Casper, Wyoming
ISBN 0-933849-16-8    Full Color

**WHO CAN FIX IT?**
written & illustrated by Leslie Ann MacKeen

by Leslie Ann MacKeen, age 9
Winston-Salem, North Carolina
ISBN 0-933849-19-2    Full Color

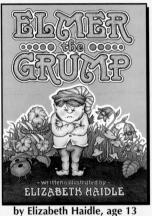

**ELMER the GRUMP**
written & illustrated by ELIZABETH HAIDLE

by Elizabeth Haidle, age 13
Beaverton, Oregon
ISBN 0-933849-20-6    Full Color

**Taddy McFinley and the Great Grey Grimly**
written & illustrated by Heidi Salter

by Heidi Salter, age 19
Berkeley, California
ISBN 0-933849-21-4    Full Color

**Problems at the North Pole**
written & illustrated by Lauren Peters

by Lauren Peters, age 7
Kansas City, Missouri
ISBN 0-933849-25-7    Full Color

**OLIVER and the OIL SPILL**
written and illustrated by ARUNA CHANDRASEKHAR

by Aruna Chandrasekhar, age 9
Houston, Texas
ISBN 0-933849-33-8    Full Color

**Life in the Ghetto**
written and illustrated by ANIKA D. THOMAS

by Anika Thomas, age 13
Pittsburgh, Pennsylvania
ISBN 0-933849-34-6    Inside Two Colors

**A STONE PROMISE BY CARA REICHEL**

by Cara Reichel, age 15
Rome, Georgia
ISBN 0-933849-35-4    Inside Two Colors

**PATULOU, THE PRAIRIE RATTLESNA[KE]**
written and illustrated by JONATHAN KAHN

by Jonathan Kahn, age 9
Richmond Heights, Ohio
ISBN 0-933849-36-2    Full Color

**ALIEN INVASIONS**
written and illustrated by BENJAMIN KENDALL

by Benjamin Kendall, age 7
State College, Pennsylvania
ISBN 0-933849-42-7    Full Color

**FOGBOUND**
written and illustrated by STEVEN SHEPARD

by Steven Shepard, age 13
Great Falls, Virginia
ISBN 0-933849-43-5    Full Color

**CHANGES**
written and illustrated by TRAVIS WILLIAMS

by Travis Williams, age 16
Sardis, B.C., Canada
ISBN 0-933849-44-3    Inside Two Colors

**A SPECIAL DA[Y]**
written & illustrated by DUBRAVKA KOLANOVIĆ

by Dubravka Kolanović, ag[e]
Savannah, Georgia
ISBN 0-933849-45-1    Full Color

# HE NATIONAL WRITTEN & ILLUSTRATED BY...AWARD WINNERS

by Dav Pilkey, age 19
Cleveland, Ohio
BN 0-933849-22-2    Full Color

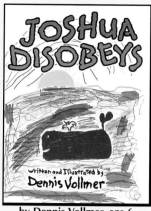

by Dennis Vollmer, age 6
Grove, Oklahoma
ISBN 0-933849-12-5    Full Color

by Lisa Gross, age 12
Santa Fe, New Mexico
ISBN 0-933849-13-3    Full Color

by Stacy Chbosky, age 14
Pittsburgh, Pennsylvania
ISBN 0-933849-14-1    Full Color

by Michael Cain, age 11
Annapolis, Maryland
BN 0-933849-26-5    Full Color

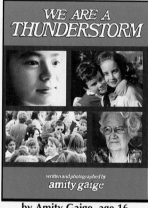

by Amity Gaige, age 16
Reading, Pennsylvania
ISBN 0-933849-27-3    Full Color

by Adam Moore, age 9
Broken Arrow, Oklahoma
ISBN 0-933849-24-9    Inside Duotone

by Michael Aushenker, age 19
Ithaca, New York
ISBN 0-933849-28-1    Full Color

by Jayna Miller, age 19
Zanesville, Ohio
N 0-933849-37-0    Full Color

by Bonnie-Alise Leggat, age 8
Culpepper, Virginia
ISBN 0-933849-39-7    Full Color

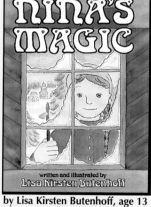

by Lisa Kirsten Butenhoff, age 13
Woodbury, Minnesota
ISBN 0-933849-40-0    Full Color

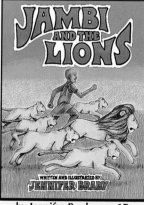

by Jennifer Brady, age 17
Columbia, Missouri
ISBN 0-933849-41-9    Full Color

y Amy Jones, age 17
Shirley, Arkansas
0-933849-46-X    Full Color

by Shintaro Maeda, age 8
Wichita, Kansas
ISBN 0-933849-51-6    Full Color

by Miles MacGregor, age 12
Phoenix, Arizona
ISBN 0-933849-52-4    Full Color

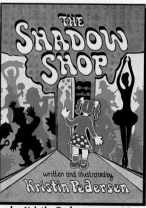

by Kristin Pedersen, age 18
Etobicoke, Ont., Canada
ISBN 0-933849-53-2    Full Color

Travis Williams
age 16

Anika D. Thomas
age 13

Isaac Whitlatch
age 11

Elizabeth Haidle
age 13

Miles MacGregor
age 12

Jayna Miller
age 19

Jonathan Kahn
age 9

Stacy Chbosky
age 14

David McAdoo
age 12

Amity Gaige
age 16

**by Laura Hughes, age 8**
Woonsocket, Rhode Island
ISBN 0-933849-57-5    Full Color

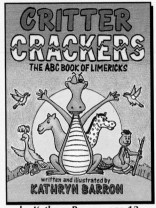

**by Kathryn Barron, age 13**
Emo, Ont., Canada
ISBN 0-933849-58-3    Full Color

**by Taramesha Maniatty, age 15**
Morrisville, Vermont
ISBN 0-933849-59-1    Full Color

**by Lindsay Wolter, age**
Cheshire, Connecticut
ISBN 0-933849-61-3    Full Color

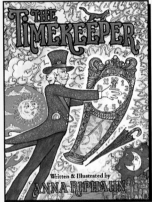

**by Anna Riphahn, age 13**
Topeka, Kansas
ISBN 0-933849-62-1    Full Color

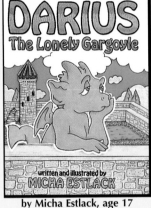

**by Micha Estlack, age 17**
Yukon, Oklahoma
ISBN 0-933849-63-X    Full Color

**by Alexandra Whitney, age 8**
Eugene, Oregon
ISBN 0-933849-64-8    Full Color

**by Gillian McHale, age**
Doylestown, Pennsylvania
ISBN 0-933849-65-6    Full Color

**by Taylor Maw, age 17**
Visalia, California
ISBN 0-933849-66-4    Full Color

**by Drew Carson, age 8**
Roseburg, Oregon
ISBN 0-933849-68-0    Full Color

**by Erica Sherman, age 12**
Westerville, Ohio
ISBN 0-933849-69-9    Full Color

**by Justin Rigamonti, age**
Hillsboro, Oregon
ISBN 0-933849-70-2    Full Color

# Written & Illustrated by... by David Melto

This highly acclaimed teacher's manual offers classroom-proven, step-by-instructions in all aspects of teaching students how to write, illustrate, assem and bind original books. Loaded with information and positive approaches really work. Contains lesson plans, more than 200 illustrations, and suggested a tations for use at all grade levels – K through college.

**The results are dazzling!**
– Children's Book Review Service, Inc.

**...an exceptional book!**
Just browsing through it stimulates excitement for writing.
– Joyce E. Juntune, Executive Director
American Creativity Association

**A "how-to" book that really works!**
– Judy O'Brien, Tea

**WRITTEN & ILLUSTRATED BY...** provi
current of enthusiasm, positive thin
and faith in the creative spirit of child
David Melton has the heart of a teache
– THE READING TEAC